PROMISES
a n d
PRIORITIES

PROMISES
a n d
PRIORITIES

52
REMINDERS FOR MEN

H. Norman Wright

VINE
BOOKS
Servant Publications
Ann Arbor, Michigan

Vine Books is an imprint of Servant Publications especially designed
to serve evangelical Christians.

Published by Servant Publications
P.O. Box 8617
Ann Arbor, Michigan 48107

97 98 99 00 01 10 9 8 7 6 5 4 3 2 1

Printed in the United States of America
ISBN 1-56955-018-2

LIBRARY OF CONGRESS CATALOGING-IN-PUBLICATION DATA

Wright, H. Norman
Promises and priorities : 52 reminders for men / H. Norman Wright.
    p.   cm.
Includes bibliographical references.
ISBN 1-56955-018-2
1. Men—Prayer-books and devotions—English.   2. Devotional calen-
dars.   I. Title.
BV4843.W747   1997
242'.642—dc21   96-51987
                                                                        CIP

CONTENTS

INTRODUCTION

IF YOU'RE LIKE ME, you prefer to read things that are brief and to the point. *Promises and Priorities* is just that. Solution-oriented, it focuses on issues that most of us as men deal with all the time. Each reading offers some practical suggestions so what you read can be applied and make a difference in your daily life.

What's the best way to use this book? You may want to select the same day each week to read the selection. But don't close the book and put it away. If you really want to capture the thought and Scripture in your life, read it over again and again. Perhaps even each day for a week. You'll be amazed at what you learn and retain. And if you read it out loud, I think you'll be surprised at the result in your retention level. It really works!

You may want to get together with a couple of other men who are also working through this resource. Sharing the thought and application can give you added strength.

God's promises were given to help us. And in today's world we need all the assistance we can receive. I hope this book is an encouragement to you and to your walk with the Lord.

H. Norman Wright

1

WALKING IN INTEGRITY

We need men of integrity today, but it's a costly virtue. You can count on it. What will it cost you? Just a few things like time, effort, money, and perhaps even popularity and respect from the people around you. Integrity isn't popular. It makes some people uncomfortable.

The word *integrity* means to be "sound, complete, without blemish, crack, or defect." In the construction business the concept of integrity refers to building codes that ensure the building will end up being safe. To have integrity the building has to be properly designed, comply with all the building codes, be safe, and be able to function in accordance with its purpose. Webster's dictionary has a simple word for it— honesty.

Get used to the word *integrity*. It's the hallmark of a righteous man.[1]

FOR REFLECTION

Do others see me as a man of integrity? In what areas do I need some work?

GOD'S PROMISE

The man of integrity walks securely, but he who takes crooked paths will be found out.

PROVERBS 10:9

MY PRIORITY & ACTION

I want to increase my level of integrity at work, with my family, and with my friends. One specific area in which I struggle with honesty is.... This week I will identify and make right one matter in my life where I have allowed dishonesty to persist.

PRAYER STARTER

Dear God, you value integrity and want me to live a life of honesty. It's difficult to succeed in this area on my own so I'm asking you to give me strength to live according to your Word, regardless of circumstances or the responses of others.

2

INCREASING YOUR EFFECTIVENESS

Would you like to get more out of your life, enjoy it more, feel relaxed, and be productive? If you said yes, consider these suggestions.

Begin each day by asking God to help you prioritize those items that need to be done. Do only those items for which you really have time. If you feel you can accomplish five during the day, do only four. Try to accomplish only one thing at a time.

Each day think about the cause for any potential time urgency. Write down one of the consequences of being in a hurry. If you begin to feel pressured about completing your tasks, ask yourself: *Will completing this matter three to five years from now? Must it be done now? If so, why? Could someone else do it? If not, why?*

Make a conscious effort to become a "ready listener" (see James 1:19, AMP). Ask questions to encourage others to continue talking. When someone is talking, put down your newspaper, magazine, or work and give that person your full attention.

Reevaluate your need for recognition. Instead of looking for the approval of others, tell yourself in a realistic way, "I did a good job and I can feel all right about it."[2]

FOR REFLECTION

Have I been following these four suggestions in my life? How?

GOD'S PROMISE

The fruit of righteousness will be peace; the effect of righteousness will be quietness and confidence forever.   ISAIAH 32:17

MY PRIORITY & ACTION

I want to live each day more effectively by practicing these four suggestions. Each day this week I will prioritize my tasks. When I feel rushed, I will stop and note the reason why. I will listen to another person without interruption, giving them my full attention, and I will speak appropriate words of approval to myself.

PRAYER STARTER

Lord, these four steps I've committed to are difficult and I need your strength to accomplish them. Help me to slow down and to remember that you are God.

STRIVING FOR THE TOP

The pursuit of position in our society is accepted as normal. We all want to move up the ladder. Each rung gets us closer to the top. But as we climb we need to ask ourselves several questions. What rung of the ladder does God want us on?

We are called to live a life of excellence. That's great. But that doesn't always mean we'll get the best position.

What's the cost of striving for position? Solomon went after prestige, power, and position, and he knew what it was like to reach the top. He couldn't go any higher. He was top dog. He was even greater than his own father. But it cost him—not just the nation but also his son Rehoboam. Scripture says, "He [Rehoboam] did evil because he had not set his heart on seeking the Lord" (2 Chr 12:14). That's a high price to pay for being on top.[3]

FOR REFLECTION

What am I striving for and what is it costing me to get there?

GOD'S PROMISE

You know that the rulers of the Gentiles lord it over them, and their high officials exercise authority over them. Not so with you. Instead whoever wants to become great among you must be your servant, and whoever wants to be first must be your slave—just as the Son of Man did not come to be served, but to serve and to give his life as a ransom for many.

MATTHEW 20:25-28

MY PRIORITY & ACTION

I want to evaluate what I am striving for in light of what God wants for me. I will write down a type of power, prestige, or position I am striving to achieve and in prayer ask God to shape my desires to match what he wants me to do for his kingdom.

PRAYER STARTER

Dear God, instead of my striving to climb the ladder to the top, place me where you want me to serve you. Enable me to be satisfied where you want me to be for your kingdom's sake.

4 USING TIME WISELY

You're probably quite conscious of time. Most of us are. Our lives are regulated by it. When you get up, eat, begin work, leave for church... it's all regulated by time. Some of us control it and others are controlled by it.

Do you struggle with time? You know, do you usually run late? Do you feel your stomach muscles tighten up when you're running behind? Or does irritation creep in when your wife keeps you waiting for twenty minutes?

There are a few things to remember about time.

Time is limited. You have 1,440 minutes a day—no more, no less.

Once you use time, it's gone. Forever. There's no retrieval system.

Time needs to be used wisely. As one man put it, "The great use of life is to spend it for something that will outlast it."

How do you use your time? Wait a minute. Let's correct that. It's not our time. It's God's. He's given it to us. So how are you using God's time?[4]

FOR REFLECTION

Who is in control of how I use my time? Me, others, the clock, or God?

GOD'S PROMISE

"Wake up, O sleeper, rise from the dead, and Christ will shine on you." Be very careful, then, how you live—not as unwise but as wise, making the most of every opportunity, because the days are evil.   EPHESIANS 5:14b-16

MY PRIORITY & ACTION

I want to use my time wisely. Each day this week I will keep track by the hour of how I spend my time. Each evening I will evaluate whether I spent the day effectively.

PRAYER STARTER

Heavenly Father, keep me from being a prisoner of the clock and self-imposed schedules. Help me to control my time and use it meaningfully.

PURPOSE IN PRAYER

All prayers are answered, but not always the way we had hoped or in the time we anticipated. We often judge the efficacy of prayer by whether it produces the results we prayed for. We make God our celestial errand-boy.

Because God can see what we cannot see, and know dimensions that we can never understand, he works out our answers according to a higher plan than we can conceive. We are to tell him our needs and then leave them with him. Only in retrospect will we be able to see the narrowness of our vision, and see that his answer was far better than what we ever could have anticipated.

Prayer is not just the place and time we tell God what to do. It is the experience in which he molds our lives.[5]

FOR REFLECTION

What is my purpose in prayer? What do I want to be different when I'm finished praying?

GOD'S PROMISE

Which of you, if his son asks for bread, will give him a stone? Or if he asks for a fish, will give him a snake? If you, then, though you are evil, know how to give good gifts to your children, how much more will your Father in heaven give good gifts to those who ask him.

MATTHEW 7:9-11

MY PRIORITY & ACTION

I want to look at the purpose and content of my prayers. This week I will begin making a list of my prayer requests and keep track over the next 90 days of how and when God answers them.

PRAYER STARTER

Dear God, help me to pray according to your will and for your purposes in our world today.

6

WHERE DO YOU FIT IN?

Have you ever felt like you didn't fit in? You know, sort of part of a group, but not really? It's an uncomfortable feeling, but it's normal if you're a Christian. When you follow Jesus, you won't really feel like you fit in… or at least you shouldn't. There's a good reason for that. You're an alien, a stranger just visiting this world for a while. Earth may be where you're living, but it's not really your home.

We are here on a visit and we have a purpose: to enjoy God as well as to love him forever, but also to help enlarge the kingdom of God. If you want an opportunity to introduce others to the kingdom, the next time someone asks you where you live, just tell them you're an alien on a visit and they wouldn't believe where your real home is.[6]

FOR REFLECTION

Am I fitting into the world too well? If so, what does this say about me?

GOD'S PROMISE

All these people [Abel, Enoch, Abraham] admitted... if they had been thinking of the country they had left, they would have had opportunity to return. Instead, they were longing for a better country—a heavenly one. Therefore, God is not ashamed to be called their God, for he has prepared a city for them.

HEBREWS 11:15-16

MY PRIORITY & ACTION

I want the way I live to reflect that I am a citizen of God's kingdom, not of this world. This week I will read Philippians 3:20, Ephesians 2:19, Colossians 3:1-4, and 1 Peter 2:11, and change a behavior in one area of my life that shows I am a stranger to this world and a member of God's kingdom.

PRAYER STARTER

Dear God, help me to remember that this is not my world. I am a temporary resident here. Keep me from becoming too comfortable with this life.

7

LIGHTEN UP WITH LAUGHTER

Being around some men is a downer. They're not much fun. They're full of gloom. They have no joy, no laughter, no life. Sure, life is tough, but there is also a lot to smile about, a lot to laugh at. Did you ever wonder what made Jesus laugh? Probably a lot of the same humorous things we enjoy.

What is it you joke about? What makes you really laugh? Where is your sense of humor displayed? At home or at work?

How do other people view you? Are you someone who can laugh easily, who exudes joy? Or are you a gloom machine? Do others think you need to "lighten up"? God is the author of smiles, joy, and laughter. He wants us to experience these gifts, express them, and infect other people with their positive potential. It's one of his prescriptions designed to make life bearable.[7]

FOR REFLECTION

Do I bring a sense of relief and laughter into the lives of those around me?

GOD'S PROMISE

A cheerful heart is good medicine....

PROVERBS 17:22

MY PRIORITY & ACTION

I want to develop a healthy balance in my attitude, between my serious side and my humorous side. Each day this week I will discover and note something to smile about, to laugh about, and to be joyful over. I will share my "cheerful heart" in a way that builds up another and honors the Lord.

PRAYER STARTER

Father, thank you for the gifts of laughter and a joyful spirit. Help me to be a source of joy to others, especially to my family. Keep me from laughing at or telling jokes that detract from my Christian walk.

8

EXPERIENCING GOD'S PLEASURE IN WORK

What part does work play in your life? Perhaps these questions can help you evaluate the place of work in your life.

Do you spend a lot of time thinking about the satisfaction you're receiving from your job, or what you wish would happen?

In what way is your job furthering the kingdom of God here on earth? If your job were taken away from you for the next six months how would you feel about yourself?

If someone asked you to explain how you experience God's pleasure in your work, what would you say?

Remember Eric Liddell in the Oscar-winning movie, *Chariots of Fire*? Everything Liddell did was for the glory of God. His sister felt he was neglecting his calling as a missionary to China, and one day she was upset with him because he missed a missions meeting. Eric said to her, "Jennie, you've got to understand. I believe God made me for a purpose—for China. But he also made me fast! And when I run, I feel his pleasure."

Can you say that about what you do?[8]

FOR REFLECTION

What part does work play in my life?

GOD'S PROMISE

Whatever you do, work at it with all your heart, as working for the Lord, not for men, since you know that you will receive an inheritance from the Lord as a reward.

COLOSSIANS 3:23-24a

MY PRIORITY & ACTION

I want to evaluate my work in light of God's call on my life. Each day I will reflect on one of these four questions. At the end of the week I will determine one new way I can make my work count for God's kingdom.

PRAYER STARTER

Dear God, help me not to distort your gift of work. Keep me from being a "work junkie" or using my work as a source for my identity.

9 LIVING THE GOOD LIFE

We all have four choices regarding "money life-style." Some choices have better consequences than others.

You can live *above* your means—that's easy. Anyone can do it. We look rich to other people. We accumulate as much as we want in goods... and pay more than we should in high interest rates.

Living *at* your means is a better choice, but still not a good one. It comes in one hand and goes out the other at the same rate. At least there's not much debt. But there are no savings, either.

Living *within* your means follows the scriptural teaching of being a good steward of what God has entrusted to you. The man who lives within his means thinks about today and the future. But more than that, he looks at how his money can be used for the kingdom of God. Tithing is a part of this man's life, even when he can't afford it.

Living *below* your means is not a typical choice. It requires unusual self-discipline and a deliberate choice not to move up. The gift of giving rather than acquiring is this man's joy. He simply uses only what's necessary.

So, there you have it.

Which of these four styles describes your life? And... is it by choice?[9]

FOR REFLECTION

Which of the various money life styles have I lived?

GOD'S PROMISE

Remember this: Whoever sows sparingly will also reap sparingly, and whoever sows generously will also reap generously. Each man should give what he has decided in his heart to give, not reluctantly or under compulsion, for God loves a cheerful giver. And God is able to make all grace abound to you, so that in all things at all times, having all that you need, you will abound in every good work.   2 CORINTHIANS 9:6-8

MY PRIORITY & ACTION

I want to use my money in keeping with what God wants. I will read Malachi 3:8-12, 2 Corinthians 9:6-8, and Mark 8:36 and decide on one new way to spend my money.

PRAYER STARTER

Dear God, my money doesn't belong to me but to you. Empower me to be a wise steward of your funds.

10 A GOOD NAME

When you're not around and other people bring up your name, what's the first thing that comes to their minds about you? Most of us will never know for sure. But it would be interesting to find out. What others are thinking and saying about us is based upon what we've let people know about us as well as how we've acted around them. We have a reputation. It follows us in the minds of others, even when we're not there. Webster's defines it as "estimation in which a person or thing is commonly held, whether favored or not; character in the view of the public."

Everyone has a reputation, whether or not we want one. A good reputation is made—it's earned. It takes hard work, and consistency of word and deed.

How's your reputation?
- To your coworkers?
- To your wife?
- To your children?
- To the Lord?

May you be well thought of![10]

FOR REFLECTION

Is God pleased with my reputation?

GOD'S PROMISE

Let love and faithfulness never leave you; bind them around your neck, write them on the tablet of your heart. Then you will win favor and a good name in the sight of God and man.

PROVERBS 3:3-4

MY PRIORITY & ACTION

I want to evaluate my reputation in light of Scripture and the people around me. This week I will ask one person (coworker, wife, or child), "In your eyes, what is my reputation?" and, based on their feedback, change one attitude or behavior to be more like Jesus.

PRAYER STARTER

Dear God, give me the strength to live my life so that others want to know about you. Help me to be more concerned about what you think of me than what others think.

11

Nothing, absolutely nothing is to come before God. The first commandment is plain and simple... and easy to break. Today gods have multiplied. Some worship the earth. Many worship Elvis and his memory. Everyone today has a god, whether they call it God or not. A famous preacher from years ago, G. Campbell Morgan, said:

> It is as impossible for a man to live without having an object of worship as it is for a bird to fly if it is taken out of the air. The very composition of human life, the mystery of man's being, demands a center of worship as a necessity of existence. All life is worship... The question is whether the life and powers of man are devoted to the worship of the true God or to that of a false one.

What you place first in your life may be your god. It could be your job, wife, golf, an accumulation of the things that make up the good life, or sex. Anything that takes priority over God has removed him from the throne. When God said you shall have no other gods before me, he was saying you shall have ME![11]

FOR REFLECTION

What takes first place in my life?

GOD'S PROMISE

But seek first his kingdom and his righteousness, and all these things will be given to you as well.   MATTHEW 6:33

MY PRIORITY & ACTION

My use of time, money, and energy shows who or what has first place in my life. I will look through my past year's checkbook and calendar to assess what is taking priority and I will make one change in my life to reflect the fact that God is first in my life.

PRAYER STARTER

Dear God, I want to sweep my life clean of any clutter that is keeping you from being first in my life. Help me to worship you with my entire life.

12

RUNNING ON
THE RIGHT TRACK

Many men are into running—some run in marathons, others compete in sprints and shorter races, while still others spend their time running from the couch to the refrigerator during commercial breaks. Running can be enjoyable, but it's hard work.

If you decide to get into running, you're faced with a multitude of choices: what kind of running or race you want to be in, why you run, how long you run, how fast, and how much time you spend running.

Once you select the race to run, you're stuck. You can't deviate from the prescribed course. If you want to run on flat land, don't go into cross-country running! You now have two goals—to finish the course and, hopefully, to place first.

We also run a spiritual race, based on the way we live. Some men run the race of life on a treadmill. They'll get exercise, but they don't go anywhere. Others run a race that destroys them. It's called the "rat race."

God has a different race for us to run, and when we run that race we're not running it alone.[12]

FOR REFLECTION

Am I running well in my spiritual race?

GOD'S PROMISE

Run in such a way as to get the prize. Everyone who competes in the games goes into strict training. They do it to get a crown that will not last; but we do it to get a crown that will last forever.   1 CORINTHIANS 9:24b-26

MY PRIORITY & ACTION

I want to assess whether I am crawling, walking, or running in my spiritual journey. I will spend time this week searching the Scriptures and noting three passages that will help me move forward in my Christian life.

PRAYER STARTER

Dear God, I want to be on the right track and in motion for you—not crawling or exhausted or on a treadmill, but consistently moving ahead.

You've got a power source for your life that will outlast any Delco or Energizer battery. It is more intense than the power pack of a nuclear submarine. But it is not just a power source, it is an actual person. That's right, a person, not an "it." Too many people think of the Holy Spirit as an "it." Scripture calls him "the Spirit of truth" and reminds us that "The world cannot accept him, because it neither sees him nor knows him. But you know him, for he lives with you and will be in you" (Jn 14:17).

John calls him the Helper. He is God inside of you to help you be a man of integrity. You may think you have to handle that business transaction, that irritating business associate, or that alluring temptation by yourself, but you don't. The Holy Spirit is there—all the time.

He has a job to do.[13]

FOR REFLECTION

Have I been relying upon the Holy Spirit as the source of power in my life? In what way have I not?

GOD'S PROMISE

In the same way, the Spirit help us in our weakness. We do not know what we ought to pray, but the Spirit himself intercedes for us with groans that words cannot express. And he who searches our hearts knows the mind of the Spirit, because the Spirit intercedes for the saints in accordance with God's will.

ROMANS 8:26-27

MY PRIORITY & ACTION

I want to make use of the Holy Spirit as the power source of my life. I will begin this week by studying John 16:7, 8, and 13. Then, each day, when I face a challenge, I will call upon the power of your Holy Spirit to help me.

PRAYER STARTER

Heavenly Father, keep me aware that your Holy Spirit is a gift given to all of us who know you through Jesus. Remind me each day that your Holy Spirit is there to empower us to be different and to do great things.

14

Mercy—We have a misconception of what it means. We think it's just a matter of showing some kindness to others. Cutting a bit of slack for someone who owes us, giving someone more time to pay off a debt, or giving a little more in the special missions offering to help the poor. This is our idea of being merciful. But that misses the mark.

The original word for mercy translates a bit differently. We do know that it doesn't simply mean to feel sorry for someone in trouble. It's the ability to get inside the other person's skin and see life with their eyes and feel things with their feelings. Mercy will cost you. It's empathy—experiencing with another person what they are going through. You're with them. It means reaching out to others in need to the extent that it costs you. You get involved—that's the key word, involved. Listen to God's Word.[14]

FOR REFLECTION

Am I a merciful person? In what ways and to whom have I demonstrated mercy recently?

GOD'S PROMISE

Blessed are the merciful, for they will be shown mercy.   MATTHEW 5:7

MY PRIORITY & ACTION

I want to practice showing mercy to others and not allow any prejudice I may have to block my ability to reach out. This week I will find someone in need and become involved in helping them to the extent that it costs me something.

PRAYER STARTER

Dear God, be merciful to me for I am a sinner. Give me a heart of mercy toward others.

15

CONSISTENT EFFICIENCY

Let's meddle a bit. What does your garage look like? What about the work room, the backyard, or the "catch-all" drawer in the kitchen? If you're married, how would your wife rate you on efficiency around the homestead? Yeah, you're right. Bad question! But necessary to ask. Why? Simply because a number of men have MPP—Multiple Personality Problem. They're super-charged workhorses on the job, but at home they function like sluggards. And to make matters worse (much worse!), if their wives know they're giving it their all at the office, they will not be happy receiving only the leftovers at home.

So what's the answer? Consistent efficiency—at work and at home. Don't try to catch up or do it all at once. Space out the chores in an orderly fashion and watch the change—in you and in your wife.[15]

FOR REFLECTION

Is there any area in my life where I could be more efficient and organized? If I asked my wife or best friend this question, what would they say?

GOD'S PROMISE

Husbands, in the same way be considerate as you live with your wives, and treat them with respect as the weaker partner and as heirs with you of the gracious gift of life, so that nothing will hinder your prayers.... For, "Whoever would love life and see good days must keep his tongue from evil and his lips from deceitful speech. He must turn from evil and do good; he must seek peace and pursue it. For the eyes of the Lord are on the righteous and his ears are attentive to their prayer, but the face of the Lord is against those who do evil."   1 PETER 3:7, 10-12

MY PRIORITY & ACTION

I want to develop the habit of being efficient at home, at work, and at church. One area of my household that needs more focused attention and energy is.... What I will do about it this week is....

PRAYER STARTER

Dear Lord, help me to develop consistency in the way I take care of my responsibilities at home, at work, and at church. Help me to save some energy from my work life for my home life and to respond to needs there in such a way that I do not have to be nagged or reminded.

16

GOD SEES BEYOND OUR FAILURES

How does God see our failures? They don't ever surprise him. He knows we will fail, and he loves us anyway. That's good news in this competitive world!

When we fail, we may be tempted to blame someone or something, but let's leave God out of the loop. He doesn't cause our failures. He simply allows them to occur.

Some failures involve sin. Some do not. No matter what, God has promised never to leave us, forsake us, or turn his back on us.

God fully understands what we can learn from our failures. He wants us to know that in each failure lies a seed of growth.

Perhaps the best news of all is that he sees *beyond* our failure. He's not stopped by what is. We may say, "Look how I've blown it. I can never be used again." God says, "Look how you've blown it. Let's discover what you can learn through this and put it to use for my kingdom." We look at our lives through a microscope. God looks at our lives with binoculars and says, "I wish you could see what I see for you in the future. I wish you could know what I know about your future." Now if that doesn't give you hope, nothing will![16]

FOR REFLECTION

Do I make use of my failures in such a way that I become a better man?

GOD'S PROMISE

'So do not fear, for I am with you; do not be dismayed, for I am your God. I will strengthen you and help you; I will uphold you with my righteous right hand.... Do not be afraid, O worm Jacob, O little Israel, for I myself will help you,' declares the Lord, your Redeemer, the Holy One of Israel."   ISAIAH 41:10,14

MY PRIORITY & ACTION

I want to accept my failures, view them as God does, and discover new ways to make use of them. This week I will recall and write down a recent failure and three things I learned as a result of it.

PRAYER STARTER

Dear God, thank you for your patience and acceptance. Teach me to say when I fail, "All right, I blew it that time. I will learn from this experience and do it differently next time."

17

ANGER:
THE GREAT COVER-UP

Do you ever get angry? Ridiculous question, isn't it? We all do. Some people show it, others stow it. Some people use it, others abuse it. Some people see it as a tool from Satan, others see it for what it is... a gift from God. You probably never heard it put that way before. But it is a gift. We need the emotion of anger. We need it to counter injustice.

We tend to view anger as a problem, but the problem is in how we use it and express it. Often our anger is a cover-up for other feelings like hurt, fear, and frustration. When you're angry, ask yourself if you're frustrated or hurt or afraid. Then deal with the real issue.

God's Word can help you use your anger wisely. "Better a patient man than a warrior, a man who controls his temper than one who takes a city" (Prv 16:32). Following the advice of this verse helps you focus and direct the power and energy of your anger.[17]

FOR REFLECTION

How do I use my anger for good and how do I misuse it?

GOD'S PROMISE

My dear brothers, take note of this: Everyone should be quick to listen, slow to speak and slow to become angry, for man's anger does not bring about the righteous life that God desires. Therefore, get rid of all moral filth and the evil that is so prevalent, and humbly accept the word planted in you, which can save you.

JAMES 1:19-21

MY PRIORITY & ACTION

I want to discover what causes my anger and learn how to express it constructively, not destructively. This week I will plan in advance and rehearse saying a constructive phrase I will use to express my anger the next time it happens. At that time of my anger, I will identify and write down my underlying feelings.

PRAYER STARTER

Dear God, I thank you for the unique way you've created me. Give me insight into the causes of my anger, the sensitivity to know its effect on others, and the ability to express it constructively.

18

HEALING A TROUBLED HEART

Many men die of heart trouble. But others die of a troubled heart. You probably won't see "troubled heart" listed on a death certificate, but it ought to be. It's real. Sometimes a friend will come up and say, "You look like your heart is troubled." It usually shows, not in chest pains, but in your face and body language.

What are the symptoms of a troubled heart? How about *anxiety*? You know, that sense of tension and of feeling wired. It's often brought on by worry. And it does a real number on us. "An anxious heart weighs a man down, but a kind word cheers him up" (Prv 12:25). You actually feel as though a hundred-pound weight were pressing on your heart... and it's not indigestion.

And then there's depression—the feeling that hope has disappeared and everything is seen through a veil of gloom. Solomon talked about a "sorrowful" heart as well. "Even in laughter the heart may ache, and joy may end in grief" (Prv 14:13).

Troubled hearts can be healed. If yours is troubled, seek out a friend. If someone else is troubled, be a friend to him.[18]

FOR REFLECTION

When have I experienced a troubled heart, anxiety, or depression in my life? When have my family or friends?

GOD'S PROMISE

I have told you these things, so that in me you may have peace. In this world you will have trouble. But take heart! I have overcome the world.

JOHN 16:33

MY PRIORITY & ACTION

I want to become more aware of difficult times in the lives of my family and friends, and share my own difficult times with them. If I am anxious or depressed this week, I will admit it and seek out the help I need. If I am not, I will look for an opportunity to listen to and encourage someone who may be.

PRAYER STARTER

Heavenly Father, I need you to listen to me when my heart is troubled. I also need others to listen. Give me the courage to seek out others during these times, and help me to be a listening friend when others are struggling.

19

IF YOU ARE HUMBLE...

Jesus has a request for you and for me. It may be difficult, especially in today's world:

Jesus asks every believer to be humble. But you can't be strong-willed if you plan to be humble. You can't promote yourself and call attention to your achievements. You can't carry around your box score to show everyone how you've done. You can't rely upon yourself if you're humble.

Being poor in spirit also means that we admit we are lacking spiritually. We have a condition known as spiritual poverty. When we admit this and acknowledge our need of God, we find lasting, permanent happiness. When you put all of your trust in God, the kingdom of heaven is yours. Do you hear anyone else making such an offer?[19]

FOR REFLECTION

Do I call attention to my own achievements? Do I call attention to Jesus Christ and what he has done for me?

GOD'S PROMISE

Humble yourselves, therefore, under God's mighty hand, that he may lift you up in due time.   1 PETER 5:6

MY PRIORITY & ACTION

I want to be more aware of how often I use the word "I" or "me" and in what ways I steer conversations to focus on my achievements. This week in at least one conversation I will draw out the interests of the other person and avoid bringing up my own accomplishments until others ask me.

PRAYER STARTER

Heavenly Father, help me to be more like your Son Jesus, who humbled himself even to the death on the cross. Remind me to promote others rather than myself.

20

AVOIDING STRESS FRACTURES

Athletes know what stress fractures are. Little microscopic cracks in bones that start from the pounding we give our body. In time they enlarge and begin to hurt.

You may think stress fractures are limited to the bones, but they're not. We pound our bodies in other ways. Our schedule begins to pile up, as do the bills; we take on a coaching job, learn to eat on the run (usually junk food), try to satisfy the boss, spouse, and church. Before long our nerves have these microscopic cracks beginning. We're on edge like a tightly wound rubber band just ready to snap at whatever gets in our way.

Your spirit and your heart can be stress fractured as well. It comes from taking on and doing too much by yourself. Whoever said we were called to go through life alone? That approach will fracture your life. There's a Shepherd waiting to help you. Why don't you let him?[20]

FOR REFLECTION

What factors are contributing to the stress in my life?

GOD'S PROMISE

Do not be anxious about anything, but in everything, by prayer and petition, with thanksgiving, present your requests to God. And the peace of God, which transcends all understanding, will guard your hearts and your minds in Christ Jesus. PHILIPPIANS 4:6-7

MY PRIORITY & ACTION

Considering God's promise, I want to identify the areas of my life where I am experiencing stress and would like God to restore and refresh me. I will list and categorize this week's activities as "crucial," "very important," "important," and "good." I will mark those that could be dropped from my life and replaced with a time of rest.

PRAYER STARTER

Dear Lord, show me which activities you consider important. Teach me to have a time of quiet and rest in your presence each day.

21

RELINQUISHING CONTROL

Some men don't seem to get the message about control. They can't control everything, but they keep trying. Why? Because they must be in control of every aspect of their lives. They push, pull, persuade, manipulate, and withdraw. Yes, withdraw. Silence and withdrawal are great ways to control others.

Control is a camouflage for fear. Who wants to be afraid or even admit that you are? Not me. Not you. Fear makes you feel vulnerable.

A secure man doesn't need always to be in control. He can defer to others, ask their advice, be comfortable when someone else leads. To feel safe we go overboard by trying to control everything and everyone. There's an emptiness within us when we're insecure, but we're like a bucket with a hole in it. We can never get filled up enough, but we keep trying through control.

Control never fulfills; it never solves the basic problem. It simply perpetuates it. It never draws others closer, rather, it pushes them away.

Give God the reins of your life. Let him control you. When God is in control of your life, you'll be amazed at how much better your relationships with others will be.[21]

FOR REFLECTION

In what ways do I attempt to control my life and others? What are the fears behind this?

GOD'S PROMISE

I will instruct you and teach you in the way you should go; I will counsel you and watch over you. Do not be like the horse or the mule, which have no understanding but must be controlled by bit and bridle or they will not come to you. Many are the woes of the wicked, but the Lord's unfailing love surrounds the man who trusts in him.   PSALMS 32:8-10

MY PRIORITY & ACTION

I want to discover how fear or insecurity may be related to my need for control. I will ask one family member or friend if and how I try to control them. In the light of their answer, I will identify the fear that may be prompting my controlling behavior.

PRAYER STARTER

Lord, help me to overcome the fears that cause me to control others. Teach me to love others as you have loved me.

22

OUR REPRIEVE FROM TREASON

Some of the most famous incidents in the history of our country have been acts of treason. Books have been written and movies made recounting the incidents and their effect upon our country. Some people are still referred to as "that traitor." Treason has been defined as "a betrayal of trust or faith; violation of the allegiance owed to one's sovereign."

We're all aware of sin in our society. It's all around us. And sin is treason against who God is, what he stands for, and his law. Once you've committed treason, you cannot *not* be a traitor, and rarely are you given a pardon. It's different, though, with God: "For the wages of sin is death, but the gift of God is eternal life in Christ" (Rom 6:23). What a reprieve! The result is eternal life. Undeserved, but given anyway! The only reason anyone would ever do something like that is because of love.[22]

FOR REFLECTION

Am I aware of when I sin? How does it affect my life?

GOD'S PROMISE

But God demonstrates his own love for us in this: While we were still sinners, Christ died for us. Since we have now been justified by his blood, how much more shall we be saved from God's wrath through him! For if, when we were God's enemies, we were reconciled to him through the death of his Son, how much more, having been reconciled, shall we be saved through his life. ROMANS 5:8-10

MY PRIORITY & ACTION

I want to be aware of when I sin and realize what it means to God. This week, when I sin, I will admit it and confess it to God, calling it by name; I will not try to cover up my wrongdoing.

PRAYER STARTER

Dear God, I confess to you that I have sinned. Thank you for your forgiveness, even when I don't deserve it, and the gift of your Son, Jesus.

23

GROWING THROUGH LOSS

Life is full of bad news. Life is full of loss. Some of the losses people experience are right up there with Job. Remember him? He was the man who lost most of his money, his herds of livestock, his crops, and his servants. And then he lost not one, but all ten of his children. Usually the loss of one child tears a family apart. But ten! And finally his health crumbled. He didn't deserve this. He was an honest, God-fearing man. He was a man of integrity.

Job accepted the fact that God was in control. He acknowledged God's sovereignty. He didn't lash out in anger at God or curse him. He accepted something that's difficult for most people to accept today: God is who he is. He's in charge, even if we don't understand why things happen the way they do.

Job said his hope was in the future. We know that one day there will be a resurrection, and all problems will be over. No doubt that hope of the future helped him handle the present (see Job 42:2-4).[23]

FOR REFLECTION

What events in my life are difficult to understand? How do I handle losses in life?

GOD'S PROMISE

We know that the whole creation has been groaning as in the pains of childbirth right up to the present time. Not only so, but we ourselves, who have the firstfruits of the Spirit, groan inwardly as we wait eagerly for our adoption as sons, the redemption of our bodies. For in this hope we were saved.   ROMANS 8:22-24a

MY PRIORITY & ACTION

I want to respond to hard times and losses in a way that reflects my hope in God. This week I will study Psalm 42:11, Job 36:15, 1 Peter 5:6-11, Romans 8:18, and 2 Corinthians 4:17-18 and write down two scriptural truths that will help me face present difficulties.

PRAYER STARTER

Heavenly Father, you too experienced loss in sending your Son, Jesus, to die for our sins. Help me to face and accept my losses, grieve over them, and then give them to you. Thank you for the hope of the resurrection.

24

BEWARE OF SUBTLE EROSION

You've heard the story of the frog that was placed in a pot of cold water on the stove over a very low flame. Well, the water temperature rose so gradually that he wasn't even aware of the change. A couple of hours later he was dead, boiled to death so gradually that he never realized what was happening.

Changes can happen to us in the same way.

Deterioration is all around us. A building suddenly crumbles and people are injured and killed. "What went wrong today?" we ask. It did not just happen today. It started to give way years ago, but it was so slight that no one noticed.

Character doesn't erode overnight.

Morals don't change suddenly.

A marriage doesn't "suddenly" fall apart.

Children don't "go wild" out of the blue.

A company doesn't "suddenly" go bankrupt.

Enough said?[24]

FOR REFLECTION

Is there any area of my life that is subtly eroding?

GOD'S PROMISE

Blessed is the man who does not walk in the counsel of the wicked or stand in the way of sinners or sit in the seat of mockers. But his delight is in the law of the Lord, and on his law he meditates day and night. He is like a tree planted by streams of water, which yields its fruit in season and whose leaf does not wither. Whatever he does prospers. PSALMS 1:1-3

MY PRIORITY & ACTION

I want to become stronger in the Lord over time, not weaker. This week I will take specific steps to stop a destructive habit, reverse an eroding relationship, or restore a fruitful endeavor that I have abandoned in my life. I will tell one person about my decision.

PRAYER STARTER

Dear God, sharpen my awareness of any subtle erosion—spiritual, moral, physical, or relational—taking place in my life. Help me to make any course corrections that are necessary.

25

BUILDING HARMONY WITH HUMOR

Some men have a real gift when it comes to the fine art of insults. That's not unusual, because men's style of humor is different from women's. We use gentle insults, poke fun at one another, emphasize each other's goofs and mistakes, and throw in some sarcasm from time to time. Men enjoy putting each other down. There's nothing wrong with any of this—when it's in fun, when it's mutual, and when it's between men. Often it occurs because we care for these men. They are our friends.

Sometimes, though, our tendency to use insults and put-downs seep into our family life. Then it becomes destructive.

Often we learn sarcasm from the sitcoms and comedy shows we watch. Put-downs and comments that hurt seem to be an accepted part of our culture. But as Christians this culture is not to be our culture.[25]

FOR REFLECTION

Do I communicate using sarcasm, insults, and put-downs? Does my sense of humor hurt or tear down others?

GOD'S PROMISE

Finally, all of you, live in harmony with one another; be sympathetic, love as brothers, be compassionate and humble. Do not repay evil with evil or insult with insult, but with blessing, because to this you were called so that you may inherit a blessing.　　　1 PETER 3:8-9

MY PRIORITY & ACTION

I want to use my humor to build closer, positive relationships, not to be detrimental to others. This week I will memorize 1 Peter 3:8-9 and practice it when I am tempted to be sarcastic.

PRAYER STARTER

Father, thank you for humor. Help me to use it in a way that builds up others.

26 PUTTING DREAMS INTO ACTION

There are three different kinds of men in this world. Which one are you?

The first are those who just get along in life. They have no dreams and no plans. They live for what's going on right now. Their lives are full of the same routine day after day, week after week, year after year. You've met some of them. Sometimes you go back to your high school reunion and you come away amazed at the lives of some of your classmates. Nothing has changed. And they don't seem to want their lives to change, either.

Other men are just full of *dreams*... but that's about all. There's no action. They talk a lot and tell everyone what they want to do. But somehow those dreams never get translated into reality. If you press them on how they're going to make their plans work, you'll hear excuses and perhaps blame.

The third group of men have *dreams with action*. They are the accomplishers. They look to God for direction, strength, insight, and wisdom. If you want some examples of men like this, look in the Bible.[26]

FOR REFLECTION

What dreams have I had over the years and what has come of them?

GOD'S PROMISE

He will keep you strong to the end, so that you will be blameless on the day of our Lord Jesus Christ. God, who has called you into fellowship with his Son Jesus Christ our Lord, is faithful. I appeal to you, brothers, in the name of our Lord Jesus Christ, that all of you agree with one another so that there may be no divisions among you and that you may be perfectly united in mind and thought.   1 CORINTHIANS 1:8-10

MY PRIORITY & ACTION

I want to be a man who puts my dreams into action. If I have a current dream, I will take it to God in prayer and ask him for his direction. If I don't, I will ask God to give me the dream he has for my life. Each day this week I will spend ten minutes thinking about and planning the steps it will take to achieve my dream.

PRAYER STARTER

Dear Lord, I put my dreams into your hands and depend on you to fulfill your plans for me. Help me to be a man of action for you.

27

TWO-WAY ACCOUNTABILITY

We're all accountable to someone. It could be our employers or company CEOs. We're definitely accountable for our money through the wonderful and kind auspices of the IRS. And we're accountable to God, especially in the future.

But what about the kind of accountability you can choose to have in your life or not? I'm talking about accountability to other Christian men. I don't mean simply friendship and fellowship with them. I mean accountability—a relationship in which they can ask you and you can ask them hard personal questions so you all stay on track. We all need to answer to someone so we can reflect the presence of God in our lives in a genuine way.

Why is accountability necessary? When you don't have someone to answer to, you're more likely to blow it. It's that clear and simple. We all like to be in charge of our own lives, to be our own bosses, but we are all blind and deaf to some of our greatest areas of need. Other people can challenge us, support us, confront us, encourage us.[27]

FOR REFLECTION

Is there someone in my life to whom I am accountable?

GOD'S PROMISE

Now listen, you rich people, weep and wail because of the misery that is coming upon you. Your wealth has rotted, and moths have eaten your clothes. Your gold and silver are corroded. Their corrosion will testify against you and eat your flesh like fire.… Look! The wages you failed to pay the workmen who mowed your fields are crying out against you. The cries of the harvesters have reached the ears of the Lord Almighty. You have lived on earth in luxury and self-indulgence. You have fattened yourselves in the day of slaughter. JAMES 5:1-6

MY PRIORITY & ACTION

I want to develop a relationship which fosters fellowship, prayer, and two-way accountability. This week I will spend at least one hour sharing with and praying for a significant person in my life. I will listen to that person's suggestions for my life too.

PRAYER STARTER

Heavenly Father, ultimately what I want most is to be accountable to you and follow your path for my life. Give me the help I need to do that.

28

THE ATTRIBUTES OF GOD

What comes into your mind when you think of God? Can you describe or list the qualities or characteristics of God? Can you describe him for someone else? What comes into your mind when you think about God could be the most important thing about you. It will affect both your worship and your daily living. That's why we need to take a close look biblically at who God is.

"God doesn't ever learn a thing. He knows all things. He doesn't have to go around spying on people to discover what's going on, he knows. Remember when you were in school and struggled in some class trying to learn something? Well, God cannot learn and has never learned. He doesn't need to. He knows everything instantly. He knows everything equally well. He never wonders about anything, never discovers anything, and is never amazed by anything. He also knows all the possibilities that can happen."[28]

FOR REFLECTION

What am I doing to learn more about who the Living God really is?

GOD'S PROMISE

Seek the Lord while he may be found; call on him while he is near. Let the wicked forsake his way and the evil man his thoughts. Let him turn to the Lord, and he will have mercy on him, and to our God, for he will freely pardon. "For my thoughts are not your thoughts, neither are your ways my ways," declares the Lord. "As the heavens are higher than the earth, so are my ways higher than your ways and my thoughts than your thoughts."   ISAIAH 55:6-9

MY PRIORITY & ACTION

I want to know more about God's attributes because who he is affects my daily life. This week I will find and read a Christian book on the attributes of God.

PRAYER STARTER

Dear God, I admit that I don't know as much about you as I could. I will spend more time with you and in your Word so I can know you better.

29

Anorexia and bulimia are words associated with eating disorders. But they can also apply to our spiritual life as well. Spiritual anorexia is an aversion to feeding from the Word of God. It is impossible for a man to stand and fight in spiritual warfare if he is spiritually malnourished.

Bulimia is an eating disorder that is commonly known as the binge-and-purge syndrome. Spiritual bulimia is knowing the Word of God without *doing* it. Or as James said, it is *hearing* the Word of God without doing it. Spiritual bulimia is characteristic of those who binge on truth: it can be through books, tapes, good Bible teaching, listening to a favorite communicator on the radio. That's why the spiritual bulimic appears to be so righteous. There's just one problem. The bulimic knows the truth, but he doesn't apply it.[29]

FOR REFLECTION

Am I applying what I am learning from the Word of God to my life?

GOD'S PROMISE

Jesus replied, "If anyone loves me, he will obey my teaching. My Father will love him, and we will come to him and make our home with him."   JOHN 14:23

MY PRIORITY & ACTION

I want to apply to my life the lessons I am learning from God's Word. This week I will select one passage of Scripture and write specifically how I will live it out this week.

PRAYER STARTER

Father, give me a greater desire to search your Word and to live out what I am learning on a daily basis.

30

INTIMACY: A SLOW JOURNEY

Sometimes intimacy hurts. Vulnerability carries with it the risk of being painfully real with another person. When a man relates closely to others, he discovers a greater awareness of himself. His fears can be dissolved and a healthy level of self-acceptance has an opportunity to develop.

Some men approach intimacy with reservation, saying, "If I do start to confront my fear of intimacy and open up, I need several things to keep myself going. I need to see there are more benefits in opening up than in staying closed. I need to see it's safe to open up. I don't want any negative value judgments about what I'm sharing. Nor do I want others telling me their opinion of what I think or feel inside. I need others to tell me it's OK to do this."

Men, be encouraged that others like you are hesitant about developing intimacy in relationships. It is a slow journey. It takes work and time and it involves a level of discomfort. It means learning more and more about your feelings. And it may involve participating in a small group of men who are willing to embark upon this same journey with you.[30]

FOR REFLECTION

Have I opened up with someone recently? What were the results?

GOD'S PROMISE

And let us consider how we may spur one another on toward love and good deeds. Let us not give up meeting together, as some are in the habit of doing, but let us encourage one another—and all the more as you see the Day approaching... So do not throw away your confidence; it will be richly rewarded. You need to persevere so that when you have done the will of God, you will receive what he has promised.

HEBREWS 10:24-25, 35-36

MY PRIORITY & ACTION

I want to develop intimacy in my relationships with others, especially my wife. This week I will describe my feelings more openly than usual, even to the point of vulnerability, with one person. I will make a note of the results.

PRAYER STARTER

Lord, sometimes it's hard to be open, not only with others, but even with you. Help me to remember how vulnerable Jesus was. By the power of the Holy Spirit help me become a risk-taker in my relationships.

31

A PRESCRIPTION FOR WEARINESS

There are days when you feel like throwing in the towel. You're wiped out, exhausted, crushed, and devastated. Even Paul felt this way. He said there was a time when there was so much opposition that he was worn out. Not just worn out. He was so tired of what had gone on that he wished he were dead.

Perhaps you've felt that kind of weariness. It could be the opposition is coming from other people at work, at church, or even in your own family.

Opposition exhausts. What do you do at a time like this? May I suggest that you put into practice the three R's.

Remember. You're not alone; and there is One who is with you.

Rest. There is no substitute for allowing your body and mind to heal. Look to the One who gives you rest.

Resolve. When your strength is back, as much as possible try to resolve the differences between you and those opposing you.[31]

FOR REFLECTION

Have I recently felt exhausted and even crushed? What is the cause?

GOD'S PROMISE

He gives strength to the weary and increases the power of the weak. Even youths grow tired and weary, and young men stumble and fall; but those who hope in the Lord will renew their strength. They will soar on wings like eagles; they will run and not grow weary, they will walk and not be faint.   ISAIAH 40:29-31

MY PRIORITY & ACTION

I want to counteract weariness in my life as best I can. This week I will write out my "prescription" for weariness, detailing how I will put the three R's into practice. I will share what I am doing with someone close to me and enlist their support.

PRAYER STARTER

Dear God, keep me from letting opposition drain me of my energy. I want to remember that you are my source of strength and are with me all day long. Give me a new love for those who oppose me.

32

PREPARED FOR DIFFICULT TIMES

Have you had a good crisis lately—you know, when a whirlwind sweeps through your life, throws you around, and disrupts all of your best-laid plans? Those crises make us feel like we're in a barrel falling downhill, being thrown all about. All of us will have crises come into our lives. But except for adrenaline addicts, not too many of us really like to have our lives invaded by crises. Before crises come, it's important to burn into your memory the fact that you will have an opportunity for more spiritual growth during a crisis than at most other times. It is during a time of crisis that God wants to do something in your life. In Isaiah 43:2, it says, "I will be with you."

Will you remember that when you are discouraged? Will you remember it when you are faced with a difficult ethical dilemma at work? Will you remember it when you feel that you have nothing left to give in your marital relationship? Will you remember it when you feel that you're all alone and no one else cares? These are words of comfort that can lift us at any time.[32]

FOR REFLECTION

What crises am I facing in my life at this time? What am I learning?

GOD'S PROMISE

Fear not, for I have redeemed you; I have called you by name; you are mine. When you pass through the waters, I will be with you; and when you pass through the rivers, they will not sweep over you. When you walk through the fire, you will not be burned; the flames will not set you ablaze. For I am the Lord, your God, the Holy One of Israel, your Savior.   ISAIAH 43:1b-3a

MY PRIORITY & ACTION

I want to *grow* through crises, not merely *go* through them. I will memorize Isaiah 43:2 this week so that I will be better prepared to grow spiritually through the next time of great difficulty.

PRAYER STARTER

Dear God, thank you that you are present with me in times of crisis. I want to be open to the lessons I can learn when I go through difficult times.

33

MARKS OF A PEACEMAKER

There are a number of misconceptions about what a peacemaker is. Some think that to be a peacemaker you should:

- avoid all arguments and conflict

- be passive and nonconfrontational

- be easygoing and let others always have their way.

Not quite.

To be a peacemaker you've got to be at peace with yourself. A peacemaker is a person who doesn't add fuel to the fire when there is a conflict. A peacemaker looks for the positive and brings it out. He looks for solution-oriented alternatives. He doesn't bait others to lure them into an argument. He knows how to arbitrate in order to settle disputes.

A peacemaker watches what he says: "Pleasant words are a honeycomb, sweet to the soul and healing to the bones" (Prv 16:24).[33]

FOR REFLECTION

Do my family and friends see me as a peace-maker? Am I at peace with myself?

GOD'S PROMISE

Blessed are the peacemakers, for they will be called sons of God.   MATTHEW 5:9

MY PRIORITY & ACTION

I want to practice my peacemaking skills. This week I will find two new ways to be a peace-maker—one at work and the other at home.

PRAYER STARTER

Dear God, you have called me to be a peace-maker, and I want to be called a peacemaker by others. Thank you for the peace that knowing Jesus brings to my own life.

34

GOD'S LOVE IS SUFFICIENT

What were your parents like? Can you think back to being a preschooler? What did you think of your parents? When you were ten, what were your thoughts about your parents? When you became a teenager, your perception of your parents had probably changed radically.

Perhaps you haven't thought about your parents very much. When you were younger and defenseless you needed them to nourish and protect you. There were times when you went running to them because you were afraid or hurt. They probably came through for you... most of the time. But sometimes they were lacking. They weren't perfect. No parent is. You may have wanted them to listen to you more, love you more, or help you more.

If there is a cry inside of you for something your parents couldn't give you or do for you, that cry can be silenced. The needs of your life can be and have been met by your heavenly Father. You have been adopted by him with all—not some, but *all*—the benefits.

If you're in need of parenting, you've got it.

If you're in need of acceptance, you've got it.

If you're in need of love, you've got it.[34]

FOR REFLECTION

In what ways do I still feel in need of parenting? Of acceptance?

GOD'S PROMISE

Can a mother forget the baby at her breast and have no compassion on the child she has borne? Though she may forget, I will not forget you! See, I have engraved you on the palms of my hands; your walls are ever before me.

ISAIAH 49:15-16a

MY PRIORITY & ACTION

I want to identify any needs from my childhood that are still unmet in my life. This week I will find and study three Scriptures that refer to God as my heavenly Father and describe the benefits I have as his child.

PRAYER STARTER

Dear Lord, let your Holy Spirit show me in your Word that your love is sufficient to overcome any deficit I bring from childhood. Thank you that you love me totally and unconditionally.

35

RULES ARE FOR A REASON

Rules… and more rules. Have you ever read the section in the newspaper that tells you what laws were passed in your state capital that day? We live in a culture that wants as much freedom as possible, yet we enact so many rules. It's unnerving at times. Sometimes it seems like there are rules for the rules.

Rules and laws are there for a reason. We need boundaries. Granted, sometimes some of our laws are ridiculous, but God's laws never are. What are some of God's rules or laws that you resist? Some of us resist only in our minds, some of us flagrantly break God's laws, while others of us devise clever schemes to get around them, believing we'll never get caught. But God's laws are not given to restrict our lives and freedom. Their purpose is to give us a better life.

Are you treating some of God's laws as suggestions, or do you see that he has given them to us for our benefit?[35]

FOR REFLECTION

How do I respond to rules I don't like or agree with? Do I comply with them willingly? Begrudge them? Bend them slightly? Or flagrantly break them?

GOD'S PROMISE

Great peace have they who love your law, and nothing can make them stumble.

PSALMS 119:165

MY PRIORITY & ACTION

I want to take a closer look (as uncomfortable as it may be) at my attitude and actions toward rules and laws, especially God's. This week I will write down one law or rule I resist or break and commit to keeping it as a way of reflecting my love for Jesus Christ.

PRAYER STARTER

Dear God, sometimes I am stubborn and resist what is best for me. Help me to comply willingly with laws and rules out of love for and commitment to your authority.

36

So... the Bible says we are to be holy. But what does that mean? How do you do whatever it takes to be holy? Perhaps a good place to begin is... with lust. Yes, lust—an issue we all struggle with in one way or another.

Lust is not just noticing that a woman is sexually attractive. Lust is born when we turn a simple awareness into a preoccupied fantasy. When we invite sexual thoughts into our minds and nurture them, we have passed from simple awareness into lust. Luther put it this way: "We cannot help it if birds fly over our heads. It is another thing if we invite them to build nests in our hair."

Paul taught that training ourselves to be godly covers this area as well. In 1 Thessalonians 4:4-6, Paul says: "Each of you should learn to control his own body in a way that is holy and honorable, not in passionate lust like the heathen, who do not know God; and that in this matter no one should wrong his brother or take advantage of him. The Lord will punish men for all such sins, as we have already told you and warned you."

Remember what Job said: "I made a covenant with my eyes not to look lustfully at a girl" (Job 31:1).[36]

FOR REFLECTION

When and where do I struggle most with lust?

GOD'S PROMISE

No temptation has seized you except what is common to man. And God is faithful; he will not let you be tempted beyond what you can bear. But when you are tempted, he will also provide a way out so that you can stand up under it.   1 CORINTHIANS 10:13

MY PRIORITY & ACTION

I want to make a covenant with the Lord to commit my sexual desires to his control and, if I am married, to focus my interests on my wife.

PRAYER STARTER

Lord, thank you for the gift of sex. Help me to keep a guard over my thought life and avoid the sin of lust.

37

CRITICISM: A COURSE CORRECTION?

How do you handle it when someone takes you to task? You know, they criticize you or make "constructive suggestions." Do you enjoy it? Probably not. Does it make you feel better? Probably not. Do you usually say, "You're right. Thanks for telling me"? Probably not. But you know what? We need all the help we can get, even though most of the time we resist it.

The Bible talks about the word *reproof.* It's a Hebrew word which means "to correct or to convince." It's not always other people who correct us. It could be God's Word. A slight course correction now can prevent disaster later on. If an airliner is off course by just half a degree (which isn't much to begin with), several hundred miles later it's way off course. It's the same way with our lives.

So, when someone gives you a reproof, what is your response going to be? You have a choice. Read Proverbs 15:31. It offers some pretty good advice.[37]

FOR REFLECTION

What is my typical response when someone criticizes me?

GOD'S PROMISE

He who listens to a life-giving rebuke will be at home among the wise. He who ignores discipline despises himself, but whoever heeds correction gains understanding.

PROVERBS 15:31-32

MY PRIORITY & ACTION

I want to be open to correction and reproof, not defensive. This week I will write three phrases I can use in the future to respond to criticism without defensiveness. Next time I receive criticism or the suggestion of another, I will listen and think about what is being said, and respond appropriately.

PRAYER STARTER

Dear God, no one likes criticism, but help me accept others' suggestions as a way to grow and correct my course in life. Thank you for your Word which shows me the best way to live.

BE ON YOUR GUARD

Years ago the television viewing audience was captivated by the cop show "Hill Street Blues." After their morning briefing and just before they hit the streets, the sergeant would say to the officers, "Let's be careful out there." He was warning them to keep their guard up because the unpredictable could and would happen.

That was good advice for those police officers. It's good advice for us as well.

"Be on your guard." Be on your guard, Jesus said, against hypocrisy (see Matthew 16:6-12), against greed (see Luke 12:15), against persecution from others (see Matthew 10:17), against false teaching (see Mark 13:22-23), and above all, against spiritual slackness and unreadiness for the Lord's return (see Mark 13:32-37). "Be careful," he said in Luke 21:34, "or your hearts will be weighed down with dissipation, drunkenness, and the anxieties of life."[38]

FOR REFLECTION

In what area of life do I need to strengthen my guard?

GOD'S PROMISE

Be dressed ready for service and keep your lamps burning, like men waiting for their master to return from a wedding banquet, so that when he comes and knocks they can immediately open the door for him. It will be good for those servants whose masters find them watching when he comes. I tell you the truth, he will dress himself to serve, will have them recline at the table and will come and wait for them. It will be good for those servants whose master finds them ready, even if he comes in the second or third watch of the night.   LUKE 12:35-38

MY PRIORITY & ACTION

I want to heed God's Word and strengthen my guard in the area of....

This week I will search God's Word on this topic, pray specifically for God's help and strength, and ask for another's support in this area.

PRAYER STARTER

Heavenly Father, make me aware of where I have let my guard down and renew my strength in this area.

39

FIX YOUR EYES ON JESUS

Keep your eyes straight ahead, says the writer of Proverbs. There are some good reasons for that admonition. You've probably already figured them out. For instance, you've seen guys at the beach with their wives. They strain their necks and turn their heads frequently, checking out the abundance of bikini-clad bare skin. Have you ever noticed the expressions on the faces of their wives? Sometimes it ranges from the deepest hurt imaginable to "You check out one more woman and you're dog meat, fella." It's probably one of the greatest insults a husband could lay on his wife, to gaze at another woman while his wife watches. It sends plenty of messages to his wife—the wrong kind. Those glances should be reserved for her!

There's another reason why our eyes stray. It's called envy, and don't think this is just a problem for women. We struggle with it as well.

Whether it's golf clubs, power equipment, or the make and year of our cars, the potential for envy is there. And when it hits, just remember: you're allowing yourself to be dominated and controlled by what the other guy has. That's a worse experience than envy. And it wouldn't happen if we were looking ahead rather than to the side. Don't fix your eyes on what others have, fix your eyes on Jesus, the author and finisher of our faith.[39]

FOR REFLECTION

Do my eyes stray? What is the reason?

GOD'S PROMISE

Do not love the world or anything in the world. If anyone loves the world, the love of the Father is not in him. For everything in the world—the cravings of sinful man, the lust of his eyes and the boasting of what he has and does—comes not from the Father but from the world. The world and its desires pass away, but the man who does the will of God lives forever.

1 JOHN 2:15-17

MY PRIORITY & ACTION

I want to increase my awareness of what I look at and what I'm thinking about at that time. This week, I will memorize Proverbs 4:25-27. When my eyes stray to what others have, I will recite this scripture and fix my eyes on Jesus.

PRAYER STARTER

Dear God, make me aware of what I am looking at and why. I want my inward thoughts to glorify you.

40

A FEW WELL-CHOSEN WORDS

Often at funerals and memorial services one or more family members or friends deliver a eulogy. They share the positive qualities, characteristics, and accomplishments of the deceased. They extol the person's virtues and go into detail as to why the person will be missed. Sometimes you wonder if they knew while they were alive that this is how others felt about them. You wonder how much of what was shared at the memorial service was ever told to them directly. In most cases, it probably wasn't.

So many parents and children end up saying, "If only I had told them how much I loved them, what I appreciated, how much they meant to me..."

"If only..." words of regret and sadness over missed opportunities. The presence of positive words can motivate, encourage, and lift up. The absence, well, perhaps they would never know what they missed. Or they could have been living with the longing for a few well-chosen words. We can't change the times we've missed, but we can fill our family members' lives now and in the future. Who needs words of love and encouragement from you? And who do you need to hear from? What others hear from you may help them do likewise.[40]

FOR REFLECTION

Who are the people in my life that need to receive a word or letter of encouragement?

GOD'S PROMISE

Pleasant words are a honeycomb, sweet to the soul and healing to the bones.

PROVERBS 16:24

MY PRIORITY & ACTION

I want to encourage the people in my life. I will give at least three statements of praise and encouragement to each of my family members this week.

PRAYER STARTER

Dear God, thank you for your belief in me and the ways you encourage me. Help me to remember that you call me not to be a critic, but to encourage others.

41

FOLLOWING GOD'S EXAMPLE

Rest. God is saying that once a week we need to take a break. He is saying there is more to life than work. He is also urging us to follow his pattern: "For in six days the Lord made the heavens and the earth, the sea, and all that is in them, but he rested on the seventh day. Therefore the Lord blessed the Sabbath day and made it holy" (Ex 20:11). Since God is God, he didn't need to rest as we know it. He certainly wasn't worn out. He just decided to. And he wants us to.

We need rest physically. There is a rhythm to the seventh day of rest that is the best balance of work and rest, even though people have tried other plans and failed.[41]

FOR REFLECTION

How am I using the Lord's Day? Am I using it for myself or for God?

GOD'S PROMISE

Let no foreigner who has joined himself to the Lord say, "The Lord will surely exclude me from his people." And foreigners who bind themselves to the Lord to serve him, to love the name of the Lord, and to worship him, all who keep the Sabbath without desecrating it and who hold fast to my covenant—these I will bring to my holy mountain and give them joy in my house of prayer. Their burnt offerings and sacrifices will be accepted on my altar; for my house will be called a house of prayer for all nations.

ISAIAH 56:3a, 6-7

MY PRIORITY & ACTION

I want to follow God's example of taking time to rest. I will discuss the use of the Lord's Day with my family or friends to determine new ways of resting and keeping it holy. This week I will adopt at least one change discussed.

PRAYER STARTER

Dear God, you have created each and every day—for this I thank you. Help me to keep your day holy. Give me more of a desire to be with you than to be involved in other activities.

42

LOOK UP IN THE MORNING

Are you a morning person, or are you married to one? You know what they're like. They wake up bright-eyed and bushy-tailed at 6:00 A.M. (or earlier). They're ready to face the day and can't wait to start talking, even before coffee!

Some of us are just not wired that well for morning. You may feel the day ought to begin at 10:00 A.M., not 6:00! Sometimes people who are early-morning "alerts" are insensitive to other people and need to heed the admonition of Proverbs: "If you shout a pleasant greeting to a friend too early in the morning, he will count it as a curse!" (27:14, TLB).

Whether you fit the 6:00 A.M. crew or the 10:00 A.M., keep in mind there is something good that can come out of the morning: time alone with God.

Is there a better way to begin your day? Not really. If you're down and the day looks dim and dreary, you can make a choice to look up. You'll be amazed at what you see![42]

FOR REFLECTION

What is my attitude in the morning? How do I respond to others?

GOD'S PROMISE

Morning by morning, O Lord, you hear my voice; morning by morning I lay my requests before you and wait in expectation... But let all who take refuge in you be glad; let them sing for joy. Spread your protection over them, that those who love your name may rejoice in you. For surely, O Lord, you bless the righteous; you surround them with your favor as with a shield.

PSALMS 5:3, 11-12

MY PRIORITY & ACTION

I want to begin the day with the Lord rather than by myself. I will make it a point to begin each morning this week with God and to be pleasant with my family members.

PRAYER STARTER

Dear God, you are the first person I want to say hello to each morning. Thank you for always being available.

43

ARE WE ALMOST THERE?

"I almost made it. Not quite, but almost."

"I'm almost finished."

"I was just a bit behind but it should be good enough—for now."

Some people live by the "almost" creed. They never quite get in line with the program. They're just a step behind everyone else.

It's easy to do this with our Christian walk. "I almost lived for the Lord today" or "I was almost a loving husband this weekend" or "I almost made it to church Sunday, but you know, we got home late Saturday night after water skiing all day and, well, you know how it goes." We become proficient at creating and using excuses. In short, we become "almost Christians."

Are you living your life as an "almost disciple"? It's easy to do, especially in our prayer life. We "almost" believe but not enough to live by faith. *Almost*—just a simple word when it stands by itself. But put it with our faith and, well, it just doesn't belong there. It belongs with incompleteness. The life and work of Jesus were complete, definite, and thorough. And that means the benefits of his life, death, and resurrection for you are complete—not "almost."[43]

FOR REFLECTION

Am I satisfied with being "almost there"? Are there areas in my life in which I live by the "almost" creed?

GOD'S PROMISE

Serve wholeheartedly, as if you were serving the Lord, not men, because you know that the Lord will reward everyone for whatever good he does, whether he is slave or free.

EPHESIANS 6:7-8

MY PRIORITY

I want to identify areas in my work, my family, or my Christian walk where I am satisfied with being "incomplete." Each time I use the word "almost" this week I will write down what I am referring to. At the end of the week I will look at the list of "almosts" and target one area for improvement and completion.

PRAYER STARTER

Heavenly Father, thank you for what the complete work of Jesus means in my life. I want my life to reflect completeness too.

44

LOVING YOUR WIFE

Do you want to know how to love your wife? The forty-nine words in the "God's Promise" section today sum it up. Read it now. A husband loves his wife as himself. Her body is his body. Her comfort is his comfort.

Love in everyday living means not only noticing that your wife may be very different in personality and temperament, but accepting it by praising her uniqueness and learning how she will help you become a more complete and fulfilled man because of it!

Love means that if you give yourself extra energy, you give her the same. Love means that if you give yourself some leisure time, you give her your time as well. Love means you learn to adapt to your wife's uniqueness.

Ephesians 5 tells us our love is to be sacrificial love (love is like death!). It is to be sanctifying love (love that elevates). It is to be self-love (loving your wife as much as you love your own body).[44]

FOR REFLECTION

Am I loving my wife in such a way that she feels loved?

GOD'S PROMISE

Husbands, love your wives, just as Christ loved the church and gave himself up for her to make her holy, cleansing her by the washing with water through the word, and to present her to himself as a radiant church, without stain or wrinkle or any other blemish, but holy and blameless. In this same way, husbands ought to love their wives as their own bodies. He who loves his wife loves himself.   EPHESIANS 5:25-28

MY PRIORITY

I want to express my love for my wife in a way that means love to her and sacrifice for me. I will read Ephesians 5 and I will ask my wife for one new way I can show my love for her. I will do it this week.

PRAYER STARTER

Dear Lord, I want to be a man who loves my wife in a way that meets her needs and helps her feel secure.

45

CHOOSE LOVE

Love is a choice. Yes, there may be feelings of love at times, but they come and go. It is a choice—especially *agape* love. This word is used in one form or another over two hundred times in Scripture. If you're married it's the type of love that will make your marriage come alive. You can't do it on your own, though. It's difficult. You need God infusing you with this love and the strength to be consistent with it. If you want to know what it's like, look at Jesus. There are three words that describe how Jesus loves us and how we're to love others.

He loves us unconditionally. He loves you with no conditions, no restrictions. No matter how wild you are, how bad you are, how mad you are, how vile you are, he loves you.

He loves us willfully. Do you understand what this means? He loves you because he wants to love you. He wasn't forced to go to the cross for you, he chose to.

He loves us sacrificially. Sacrificial love gives all, expecting nothing in return. It's a costly love.[45]

FOR REFLECTION

Am I expressing the three elements of *agape* love at work and at home?

GOD'S PROMISE

Dear friends, if our hearts do not condemn us, we have confidence before God and receive from him anything we ask, because we obey his commands and do what pleases him. And this is his command: to believe in the name of his Son, Jesus Christ, and to love one another as he commanded us.   1 JOHN 3:21-23

MY PRIORITY & ACTION

I want to love others unconditionally, willfully, and sacrificially, as God loves me. This week I will identify one person from whom I am withholding my love because of circumstances or conditions, and I will choose to express *agape* love to him/her in a new way.

PRAYER STARTER

Dear God, I thank you for your *agape* love in my life, even though I don't deserve it. Help me to love others in an unconditional and sacrificial way.

46

THE SOUND OF SILENCE

We live in a polluted world. There are many kinds of pollution, but let's talk about one—noise pollution. You can't even go into a nice restaurant for dinner without having to contend with loud music. Noise—noise—noise—radios, TV, horns, airplanes, people talking and yelling, electric lawn mowers and blowers, freeways. Isn't there any place where there's no sound?

Can you handle the stillness of solitude? Is it unnerving to sit and listen to… nothing? Are you an activity addict? Are the noises in your head so loud you can't hear God talking to you? His still, small voice won't try to out-shout the noise. It will always be a still, small voice. He's waiting for you to be quiet, to listen, to relax, so that you can be restored.

It's difficult to become a man of God without the sound of silence.[46]

FOR REFLECTION

Do I get quiet enough to hear God speak to me? When?

GOD'S PROMISE

I do not hide your righteousness in my heart; I speak of your faithfulness and salvation. I do not conceal your love and your truth from the great assembly.   PSALMS 40:10

MY PRIORITY & ACTION

I want to reduce the noise pollution I create in my own life and spend more time in silence. Each day this week I will replace one-half hour of television or radio time with quietness.

PRAYER STARTER

Dear God, I will be quiet in your presence. Speak to me and direct my thoughts and my steps.

47

OPPORTUNITY IN FAILURE

Doesn't it get to you? Some people seem to get all the breaks. Whatever they do turns to gold. They're *always* successful. You do what they do, but it doesn't come out the same. They know the right people, have the right connections, or just "happen" to be in the right place at the right time, right? Well, not exactly, and not usually. It's easy for us to see someone else's success. What we rarely see are their failures or even their humiliations.

Most people who are successful have been knocked down again and again like a prize fighter. But they bounce back with the words "next time."

You've probably gone to Disneyland or Disney World. Years ago a man had an idea for a cartoon called "Steamboat Willie." He kept going around Hollywood trying to entice people to believe in his idea. He was bankrupt. Other people saw him as a failure. But Walt Disney kept at it! He said, "Next time." And the rest is a legend. Steamboat Willie became Mickey Mouse!

We've all failed. And that's all right. Failure brings about growth and change. It only stops us when we see it as the final chapter in life. If we see it as a detour, we can learn from it and go on.[47]

FOR REFLECTION

Do I view my failures as slight detours or as impossible barriers?

GOD'S PROMISE

Therefore we do not lose heart. Though outwardly we are wasting away, yet inwardly we are being renewed day by day. For our light and momentary troubles are achieving for us an eternal glory that far outweighs them all. So we fix our eyes not on what is seen, but on what is unseen. For what is seen is temporary, but what is unseen is eternal.   2 CORINTHIANS 4:16-18

MY PRIORITY & ACTION

I want to improve my response to failures in my life. This week I will find and read the biography of a man who grew through his experience of failure (Abraham Lincoln, Chuck Colson, Walt Disney, etc.).

PRAYER STARTER

Dear Lord, give me the resilience to bounce back from failure, the wisdom to learn through disappointment, and the strength to grow through adversity.

48

BECOMING A WHOLE MAN

Some men strive to be macho. But the world's standard of a man is a perversion of what it means to be masculine. If you want a model of masculinity, think about this portrait of a balanced man.

Jesus' personality had several facets, but he did not hide them from anyone. He chased the corrupter out of his temple in righteous anger, displaying his manhood in what might be called "masculine" ways—and yet later he wept over Jerusalem, displaying what is often considered a "feminine" side.

There is no greater picture of the "whole man"—a man who was "masculine" in terms of strength, muscle, sinew, and courage, and yet was not ashamed to show his "feminine" side in terms of tears, compassion, gentleness, and peace.[48]

Perhaps what we label as "feminine" isn't really feminine at all. It's complete masculinity.

FOR REFLECTION

In what ways does my life match up with the "masculine" and "feminine" sides of Jesus?

GOD'S PROMISE

It was he who gave some to be evangelists, and some to be pastors and teachers, to prepare God's people for works of service, so that the body of Christ may be built up until we all reach unity in the faith and in the knowledge of the Son of God and become mature, attaining to the whole measure of the fullness of Christ.

EPHESIANS 4:11-13

MY PRIORITY & ACTION

I want my beliefs about masculinity to be in harmony with the kind of man Jesus was. I will read Galatians 5:22 this week, each day focusing on one fruit of the Spirit and how I can make it evident in my life.

PRAYER STARTER

Dear God, help me to be a man of strength tempered with gentleness, a man of courage coupled with compassion, and a man who can confront the wrongs of life with the heart of a peacemaker.

49

RELATIONAL BANK ACCOUNTS

What's the status of your bank account? Is there a surplus, or are you running in the red? One of the metaphors used to describe a couple's interaction is that of a bank account. There are variations of this, but one is called a Relational Bank Account.

As is true of any bank account, the balance in the Relational Bank is in flux because of deposits and withdrawals. Relationship deposits vary in size just like our monetary deposits. They could be a kind word or action or a very large gift of love. Withdrawals also vary. A minor disagreement could be a small withdrawal, but a major offense could drain the account. Zingers are definitely a withdrawal, and so is defensiveness.

When you begin thinking of your relationship in this way, you can be more aware of deposits and attempted deposits as well as what constitutes a withdrawal. Naturally, the larger the balance, the healthier the relationship. And just like a monetary account, it's best to have sufficient reserves in your Relational Bank Account. Unfortunately, many couples live with their balances at the debit level.[49]

FOR REFLECTION

Do I make more deposits or more withdrawals in my relationship with my wife and others?

GOD'S PROMISE

Be imitators of God, therefore, as dearly loved children and live a life of love, just as Christ loved us and gave himself up for us as a fragrant offering and sacrifice to God. But among you there must not be even a hint of sexual impurity, or of greed, because these are improper for God's holy people. Nor should there be obscenity, foolish talk, or coarse joking, which are out of place, but rather thanksgiving... For it is shameful even to mention what the disobedient do in secret. But everything exposed by the light becomes visible, for it is light that make everything visible. This is why it is said: "Wake up, O sleeper, rise from the dead, and Christ will shine on you."

EPHESIANS 5:1-4, 12-14

MY PRIORITY

I want to be more of a giver than a taker in my relationships. This week I will eliminate "zingers" and defensiveness from my relationships, and I will add one act of kindness each day.

PRAYER STARTER

Father, help me to learn to give to others liberally, as you have given to me.

50

Busy, busy, busy. It seems to be a characteristic of our lives. And if we're real accomplishers, those around us reinforce it by saying, "I don't know how you do all you do. It's just amazing!" And we beam with pride.

You may be busy, but are you exhausted?

You may be busy, but are you enjoying what you do?

You may be busy, but what is it costing you?

These are hard but necessary questions.

Most busy people struggle with weariness, too. And if this continues over a period of time, work suffers, the desire to continue diminishes, tempers flare, patience becomes nonexistent, and soon we give up. We get tired of being tired all the time. It's not a new problem. Do you know what to do to restore the balance of your life?[50]

FOR REFLECTION

Do I have balance in my life right now? If not, why?

GOD'S PROMISE

"Come to me, all you who are weary and burdened, and I will give you rest."

MATTHEW 11:28

MY PRIORITY

I want to be aware of how my level of activity affects me emotionally, physically, mentally, and spiritually. This week I will create a list of my major activities and note which ones I enjoyed and which ones made me weary. At the end of the week I will write down one strategy to avoid becoming too tired next week.

PRAYER STARTER

Lord, sometimes I'm weary and exhausted. Restore my energy and my enthusiasm for life and for you. Show me the steps to achieve the balance you want for my life.

51

THE OTHER SIDE
OF FAILURE

Failure! The word we dread. Some of us don't allow it in our vocabularies. Failure is what happens to others, or so we hope, but it hits all of us at times.

Webster's Dictionary says failure is "the condition or fact of not achieving the desired end." But is failure just the absence of success? Is it simply a matter of bombing out, of not completing what we set out to attain? Perhaps not.

Many men have achieved significant goals, but found no satisfaction in them. This is one side of failure. It's like climbing a path up a mountain and making it to the top, only to find out you climbed up the wrong mountain! Failure is not just the pain of a loss but the pain of a new beginning as well.

Think about this perspective on failure from a Promise Keeper speaker, Dr. Gary Oliver:

> What apart from God feels like a failure can, in his skilled hands, become a part of his provision for our growth. We can't be successful in the Christian life if we deny the existence of failure. If we learn how to value it, understand it, and take it to the foot of the cross we can become wiser and stronger because of it.[51]

FOR REFLECTION

How do I respond to the failures in my life?

GOD'S PROMISE

But we have this treasure in jars of clay to show that this all-surpassing power is from God and not from us. We are hard pressed on every side, but not crushed; perplexed, but not in despair; persecuted, but not abandoned; struck down, but not destroyed. We always carry around in our body the death of Jesus, so that the life of Jesus may also be revealed in our body.   2 CORINTHIANS 4:7-10

MY PRIORITY & ACTION

How have I grown stronger through past failures? I will take time this week to thoughtfully recall two or three failures in my life and write down what I learned from each circumstance.

PRAYER STARTER

Father, you understand how I feel when I mess up. Still, you accept me. Help me to accept my own past and learn from it. It helps to know that in your hands, my failures can be turned into opportunities to grow.

52

SPEAKING THE TRUTH— REGARDLESS

The heart is an important organ. We make reference to it all the time. When we're scared we say, "My heart almost stopped with fright." If we know someone who's generous we describe him as "having a big heart." When we describe a person as having a broken heart, we are talking about grief.

When David in Psalm 15 says, "and speaks truth in his heart," he's saying a man of character is truthful and can be depended on to speak the truth regardless. There's the key word— *regardless*—regardless of how much is costs him.

Regardless of how much it makes him look bad.

Regardless of how much difficulty he gets into.

Telling the truth is rare today. Who can you count on to consistently tell the truth? Anyone? If you are that person, you'll be different from others. But you'll also be trusted. Telling the truth benefits you, but more than that, it's a way to bring honor and glory to God in today's society.[52]

FOR REFLECTION
How willing am I to be truthful with others?

GOD'S PROMISE

Lord, who may dwell in your sanctuary? Who may live on your holy hill? He whose walk is blameless and who does what is righteous, who speaks the truth from his heart and has no slander on his tongue, who does his neighbor no wrong and casts no slur on his fellow man, who despises a vile man but honors those who fear the Lord, who keeps his oath even when it hurts, who lends his money without usury and does not accept a bribe against the innocent. He who does these things will never be shaken.

PSALM 15

MY PRIORITY

I want to be a man who can be depended on to speak the truth in love, *regardless*. This week I will discuss with another Christian what it means to speak the truth in love. I will adopt and practice one new behavior as a result of that discussion.

PRAYER STARTER

Dear God, You are truth. Your Word is truth. I want to be a man of truth.

CONCLUSION

You've been through the fifty-two weeks. It's time to reflect. Which of the sessions struck a chord in your life? Can you identify changes that you have made by following the "Priority and Action" sections? Which passages from the Scripture are now a part of your life? Have there been any other men influenced by you as you shared these readings together?

Reflect on these questions. Even though you've concluded these readings, you're not finished yet. It's time to begin at the beginning of the book and take the journey a second time. You'll be amazed at what you will find new this second time through. Remember, God's promises never change. And it's incorporating his Word into our life that enables us to keep our priorities straight.

NOTES

1. Norman Wright, *With All My Strength: Daily Devotions for Men* (Ann Arbor, MI: Servant, 1996), January 26.

2. Wright, October 22.

3. Wright, March 5.

4. Wright, March 28.

5. Wright, January 22, adapted from Lloyd John Ogilvie, *God's Best for My Life* (Eugene, Ore.: Harvest House, 1981), January 16.

6. Wright, May 16.

7. Wright, February 1, adapted from Charles R. Swindoll, *The Finishing Touch* (Dallas: Word, 1994), 64-65.

8. Wright, March 31.

9. Wright, April 26, adapted from Patrick Morley, *Seven Seasons of a Man's Life* (Nashville, Tenn: Thomas Nelson, 1990), 90-91.

10. Wright, June 1, as quoted from *Webster's New World Dictionary, Third College Edition* (New York: Prentice Hall, 1994), 1140.

11. Wright, July 20, adapted from G. Campbell Morgan, *The Ten Commandments* (New York: Revell, 1901), 18-19.

12. Wright, May 2, adapted from Joe E. Brown, *Battle Fatigue* (Nashville: Broadman and Holman, 1995), 30-36.

13. Wright, February 4, adapted from Max Lucado, *A Gentle Thunder* (Dallas: Word, 1995), 68-69.

14. Wright, April 22.

15. Wright, January 5.

16. Wright, September 2, adapted from Gary J. Oliver, *How to Get It Right When You've Gotten It Wrong* (Wheaton, Ill: Victor, 1995), 66-78.

17. Wright, March 19.

18. Wright, September 17.

19. Wright, April 14.

20. Wright, January 4.

21. Wright, March 26.

22. Wright, February 3, quoted from *Webster's New World Dictionary*, 1424.

23. Wright, January 15.

24. Wright, March 11.

25. Wright, March 10.

26. Wright, September 22, adapted from Brown, 117-18.

27. Wright, August 7.

28. Wright, August 20, adapted from A.W. Tozer, *The Knowledge of the Holy* (New York: Harper Brothers, 1961), 61-62.

29. Wright, January 21, adapted from Bill McCartney, *What Makes a Man* (Colorado Springs: NavPress, 1992) from an article by Steve Farrar, 58-59.

30. Wright, February 11.

31. Wright, August 28.

32. Wright, December 3.

33. Wright, April 24.

34. Wright, June 14.

35. Wright, February 9.

36. Wright, January 2, adapted from R.C. Sproul, *Pleasing God* (Wheaton, Ill.: Tyndale, 1988), 79.

37. Wright, February 27.

38. Wright, March 12, adapted from Gary Rosberg, *Guard Your Heart* (Portland, Oreg.: Multnomah, 1994), 15-17.

39. Wright, November 13.

40. Wright, July 5, adapted from H. Norman Wright, *Quiet Times for Parents* (Eugene, Oreg.: Harvest House, 1995), March 25.

41. Wright, July 23.

42. Wright, April 12.

43. Wright, April 1.

44. Wright, March 6, adapted from R. Kent Hughes, *Disciplines of a Godly Man* (Wheaton, Ill: Good News/Crossway Books, 1991), 42.

45. Wright, November 4, adapted from Ronnie W. Floyd, *Choices* (Nashville, Tenn.: Broadman & Holman, 1994), 112-14.

46. Wright, May 30.

47. Wright, January 10.

48. Wright, January 17, adapted from James Johnson, *What Every Woman Should Know About a Man* (Grand Rapids, Mich.: Zondervan, 1981), 104-5.

49. Wright, November 28.

50. Wright, December 1.

51. Wright, October 24, adapted from Oliver, 17.

52. Wright, February 12, adapted from John Trent and Rick Hicks, *Seeking Solid Ground* (Colorado Springs: Focus on the Family, 1995), 58-60.